GW00500069

Shipping Company Colours

Edward Paget-Tomlinson

Landmark Acknowledgements

Mike Stammers, former Director of Merseyside Maritime Museum, for writing the Introduction; Robert Shopland, former Editor of *Ships Monthly* magazine for checking the proofs; Pam Paget-Tomlinson for her kind help and assistance in the production of this book.

SHIPPING COMPANY COLOURS

Edward Paget-Tomlinson

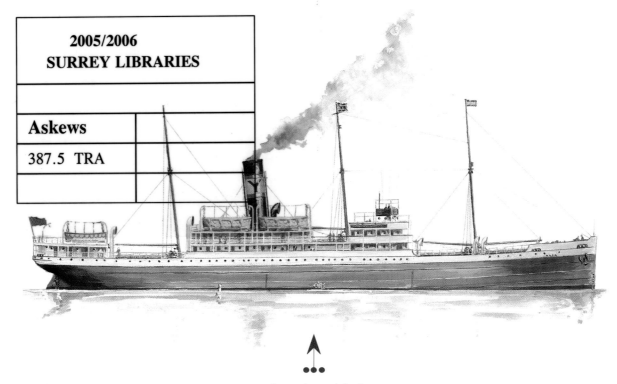

Landmark Publishing

Contents

Introduction

House flags and funnel colours made steamers distinctive in the same way that figureheads had done for sailing ships. Indeed some went back to the days of sail. T & J Brocklebank which had owned ships from the late 18th century perpetuated the same broad white band around the hull and their distinctive blue and white colours when they changed to steamers in the late 19th century. Some had nicknames. For example the Harrison Line's funnel colours included two white bands separated by a red one. This was always known as 'two of fat and one of lean'. Such markings remained more the less the same up until the end of the 1960s. By then jet air liners were depriving passenger liners of their customers and container ships were replacing conventional cargo liners. Every 'box ship' was reckoned to replace six cargo liners. The expense of buying these new ships and equipping them with containers meant that many traditional companies merged and with those mergers the old colours went. The marketing consultants were also influential in persuading shipping firms that they needed to throw out tradition and 'rebrand' with new corporate logos. There were also many new shipping companies sailing under the flags of newly independent nations or flags of convenience which took over most of the tramp trades from British companies. The result has been that by 2005 not many companies have retained their old colours. There are a few exceptions such as Cunard (owned in the United States now) and the Isle of Man Steam Packet Company. This means that this book of Edward's has a reference, an aesthetic and a nostalgic value. However the text has not been updated since Edward wrote it some ten years or so ago.

In 1956, Edward Paget-Tomlinson was appointed as a temporary curator at Liverpool Museum to produce a maritime history exhibition as part of the celebrations marking the 750th anniversary of Liverpool's first charter. The exhibition which was held at Littlewoods Social Club in Dale Street was a great success. It concentrated on the history of the major shipping companies that were still based in the port. Along with a splendid selection of models, there was a set of large shields depicting the funnel colours and house flags. I am not sure whether Edward painted these, but he certainly did produce a smaller set for a later display in the Museum. Edward was very much a practical curator, he had to be. He would turn his hand to conservation whether it was ship models or stem engines and many of the picture panels in the various shipping exhibitions during his time at Liverpool were his handiwork. One of his panels, a diagram of the first Blue Funnel liner is still on show in the *Builders of Great Ships* exhibition at Merseyside Maritime Museum.

After he left Liverpool in 1969, Edward became involved with setting up of the new Hull Maritime Museum and the Boat Museum, Ellesmere Port. You could say that the inland waterways and their distinctive types of boat were his first love. He went on to write to an award winning encyclopedia on canals and canal boats and other books and articles. He also never lost his interest in deep sea vessels. Among his many paintings and writings, he produced a set of shipping company house flags and funnel colours with potted histories attached for *Ships Monthly*. They were an attractive colour feature and full of useful information. They deserve to be re-published as a full set. Not only are they are valuable source of reference. Most flag and funnel books give you only the colours and the name of the company. Edward gives you the authoritative history as well. I know this work will be of great interest to the many people who are interested in shipping history. It is also a memorial to Edward and a reminder to all who had the privilege knowing him of how much his knowledge, artistic talent and friendship will be missed.

Although starting with sail, from 1856 under the name of the Anchor Line, the company was running passenger and cargo steamers between Glasgow and New York and tried a service to Canada. Emigrants became their main business, ably run by Thomas Henderson and his brothers, hence for a while (1859-63) the four links of the anchor cable in the houseflag to mark the four partners. Two brothers, David and William, in 1873 entered marine engineering and shipbuilding as D & W Henderson. By 1869 emigrants were collected from Scandinavia by way of Granton on the Forth and from Italy, whence they sailed from Naples to the United States. Entry into the Mediterranean trade and the opening of the Suez Canal in 1869 gave Anchor a chance to go east and a Bombay service from Glasgow via Liverpool was started in 1875, followed in 1882 by one to Calcutta.

Started in 1880 the Barrow-New York sailings were short-lived, but the Barrow-built Inman liner *City of Rome* was operated with success between Liverpool and New York from 1888 to 1891. By 1895 the Henderson brothers were dead but in 1899 the company was re-constituted under limited liability and the fleet modernised. Cunard secured a large financial stake in 1911 and in 1912 T. & J. Brocklebank bought the Calcutta business. In 1916 Anchor joined with Donaldson to form Anchor-Donaldson in the Canadian trade. Following severe war losses Anchor undertook a rebuilding programme but became overstretched and were rescued in 1935 by a syndicate which placed them under Runciman management. The Bombay service was re-equipped with motor ships headed by the *Circassia* of 1937.

Following the Second World War and more losses, the company came under the ownership of United Molasses in 1949, but remained under Runciman management. Runciman ownership followed in 1965, but the Bombay sailings ceased the following year. Thereafter bulk carriage and liquified gas transport became the company's business, the latter being their present activity with George Gibson & Co.

Many thanks to Duncan Haws for help with the preparation of picture and text.

The *Circassia* was built in 1937 by Fairfield at Govan, 11,170 gross tons, 506.6ft length overall. Twin-screw, two 8-cyl Fairfield-Doxford opposed piston engines made at Fairfield. 16$\frac{1}{2}$ knots. Took last Glasgow-Liverpool-Bombay sailing January 1966, broken up April 1966. The ship is drawn as completed in 1937 without radar.

Blue Star

William and Edmund Vestey entered the meat trade with shops and cold stores and, in 1897, formed the Union Cold Storage & Ice Co in Liverpool. Their main source of supply was the Argentine via the Royal Mail Steam Packet Co, but they and others in the River Plate trade charged high freights, so the Vesteys decided to carry their own meat and started in 1904 with chartered tonnage. Their first two owned vessels were bought in 1909 and, in 1911, they formed the Blue Star Line, employing secondhand refrigerated tonnage, although they acquired a new ship in 1914. Early ship names were prefixed 'Brod' (*Brodmount* etc), the star names started in January 1919 with *Royalstar*, split into two words from 1929, thus *Royal Star*.

War losses prompted a building programme which included the fast turbine *Doricstar* of 1921, capable of 21 knots, setting a standard for the future. Sailings to the Pacific Coast of North America were added from 1920 and New Zealand and Australia from the early 1930s. Passenger ships were introduced in 1927 between London and Buenos Aires, four and then a fifth, the *Arandora* which became the cruising liner *Arandora Star*. The *Tuscan Star* of 1930 was the company's first motor ship and a rebuilding programme followed for the Australian and New Zealand trades to designs which were maintained until 1948.

Second World War losses totalled 29 ships but the company expanded by acquiring Lamport & Holt in 1944 and the Booth Line in 1946. Transfer of ships within the group followed and further route expansion with the founding of the Austasia Line in 1952 between Malaysia, Singapore and Australia, the takeover of Donaldson's Pacific Coast services in 1954, and a joint investment in Crusader Shipping in 1957 to run between New Zealand and Japan. In 1962 the company started an Australia-USA-Canada service and, in 1964, transhipment sailings from the Continent with

coasters under the Blue Star flag. Next year a River Plate-Italian ports route was begun under the Calmedia banner.

In 1966 Blue Star joined ACT (Associated Container Transportation) with the maiden voyage of *ACT 1* in 1969 and, in 1971, the Vestey group with the Danish East Asiatic Co started the Scanstar container service to the Pacific Coast of North America, soon to be joined by Sweden's Johnson Line. In 1973 a heavy lift ship, the *Starman*, was built in association with Robert Sloman of Hamburg.

There have been more funnel and hull variants than those illustrated, notably the white hull with a red band of the *Arandora Star* and the white band of pre-war cargo liners. Grey hulls and masts and a blue waterline were introduced in 1959, when 'reefers' were given white hulls. The funnel has remained the same since 1920. The first funnel was buff with a black top, a blue star was added to the buff in 1911 and, from 1912, the buff was replaced by red, darker than at present.

Many thanks to Duncan Haws for his help.

The *Melbourne Star* was built in 1948 by Harland & Wolff at Govan, 13,179 gross tons, 572.3ft length overall. Twin-screw, two 8-cylinder Harland-Burmeister & Wain double-acting two-stroke engines, 17 knots. Sold and broken up 1972.

The *Scottish Star* was built in 1985
by Harland & Wolff at Belfast,
10,291 gross tons, 495.4ft length
overall. Single-screw, one 7-cylinder
Harland-Burmeister & Wain single-
acting two-stroke engine, 20 knots.

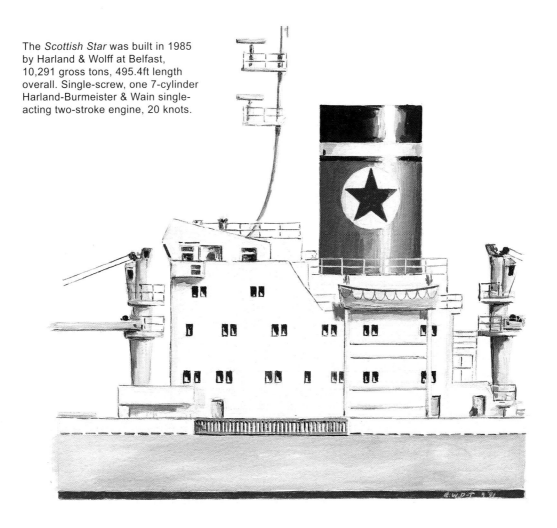

Canadian Pacific

Incorporated in 1881, Canadian Pacific's rail network reached the Pacific in 1885 but shipping links were needed with the Far East. Sailing ships and then steamers were chartered but, in 1881, the first of three 'Empresses' arrived for a Vancouver, Yokohama and Hong Kong service.

On the Atlantic, Canadian Pacific were dependent on the Allan Line but wanted their own ships. In 1903 they bought the Beaver Line from Elder Dempster and the latter's North Atlantic fleet, good for the immigrant and cattle trades, but CPR were intent on an express service. Two ships were ordered, the *Empress of Britain* and the *Empress of Ireland*. They were ready in 1906 and secured half the mail contract from the Allan Line whom Canadian Pacific were soon to control.

The *Duchess of Bedford* was built in 1928 by John Brown at Clydebank, 20,123 gross tons, 582ft length overall.

The *Empress of Britain* (III) was built in 1956 by Fairfield at Govan, 25,516 gross tons, 640ft length overall.

Well established on both oceans, Canadian Pacific maintained an up to date fleet which culminated with the *Empress of Britain* of 1931 on the Atlantic and the *Empress of Japan* of 1930 on the Pacific. London cargo services were handled by the 'Beaver' Class of turbine and turbo-electric steamers. Although the Pacific passenger sailings did not survive the Second World War, Canadian Pacific maintained the Montreal and Halifax schedules from Liverpool, replacing the *Empress of Scotland* and *Empress of France* with three new ships, the last, the *Empress of Canada* (III), appearing in 1961. 'Beaver' ships were now being built for the St Lawrence Seaway and ice navigation and, in 1970, the *CP Voyageur* arrived as their first purpose-built container ship. Tankers, bulk, chemical and forest products carriers followed and, in Canada, services were maintained on the Great Lakes, across the Bay of Fundy and in British Columbia.

The red and white houseflag was introduced in 1891 and was based on the way land was marked on the CPR railroad map, but, in 1968, a new design appeared to present a more modern corporate identity. CP Ships wore two shades of green while the ferries under the railroad had the same design in red, white and black.

Funnels were, first, buff or buff with a black top then, in 1946, the house flag was placed on the side, finally, in 1968, came the new style. White was the predominant hull colour for the

'Empresses', black for the 'Monts' and the 'Duchesses', while the green waterline has been constant. There have been variations and white, green and blue ribands have been used round the hulls.

Many thanks to Duncan Haws for guidance and to two books, *Canadian Pacific* by George Musk (David & Charles 1981) and *Mercantile Houseflags and Funnels* by J.L. Loughran (Waine Research Publications 1979).

The *CP Voyageur* was built in 1970 by Cammell Laird at Birkenhead, 15,680 gross tons, 548ft length overall.

Donaldson

Founded in 1855 by two Donaldson brothers aided by an elder brother, the first ships were barques on the Glasgow-South American run. Sixteen sailing ships were owned and chartered but, in 1870, two steamers were built, the second one starting Donaldson's summer Glasgow-Canada service. Regular Canadian sailings began in 1874, to Quebec and Montreal in the summer, to Halifax and St John, New Brunswick in the winter, and the company concentrated on the import of live cattle from Canada with return cargoes of coal. There was a Baltimore service from 1880 which, from 1895, operated all the year round. Passenger ships were run to Canada from 1905. From 1910 this became a weekly service from the Clyde. Equally important was the carriage of newsprint pulp from Newfoundland to Manchester and London for the 'Daily Mail'.

First World War losses totalled nine out of thirteen but 1916 saw a business development when the Cunard-controlled Anchor Line formed with Donaldson's the Anchor-Donaldson Line to run the Canadian service. This left Donaldson's freer to concentrate on their still existing South American sailings which, in 1913, had been augmented by buying the Allan Line's service to that continent. In 1919 the Donaldson South American Line was formed jointly with John Black & Co, managers of the Glasgow Steamship Co. Frozen meat was the main business. Motor ships were introduced from 1924 and sailings extended via the Panama Canal to the Pacific Coast of North America, and to the Mexican Gulf, the latter also served from Avonmouth which Donaldson ships had used since 1894. The liquidation of the Anchor Line in 1935 left Anchor-Donaldson to be wound up and replaced by the newly created Donaldson Atlantic Line. From 1938 Donaldson's became a public company as Donaldson Brothers and Black. Certain constituents were wound up, including, in 1941, the Donaldson South American Line.

Fourteen ships were lost in the Second World War, among them

the *Athenia* on the first day. Profits had been good but, by the 1950s, the business was in decline. In 1954 the Donaldson Atlantic Line finished and the North Pacific trade was given up, but the following year the South American sailings were resumed after four years suspension. In 1957 a Great Lakes service was started from Glasgow.

The company's last new ship was the *Letitia* delivered in 1961 but returns were now low in spite of entries into aviation and packaged holidays. In 1966 passenger services were given up and the fleet was sold the next year. Blue Star, which had bought the two ships on the North Pacific run, now acquired the South American service and the Head Line secured one ship, the

Santona which continued under Donaldson management. Liquidation of the company was completed in 1970.

Funnel and hull colours were always the same except for an early (1870-74) version of the funnel, red with a white band and a black top and a narrow black band between the red and the white. But it was too similar to Glasgow's Allan Line, so the red was replaced by black. The flags also remained unaltered save for the distinguishing pendants of the subsidiaries.

The *Corinaldo* was built in 1949 by Charles Connell in Glasgow, 8,392 gross tons, 474.5ft length overall. Single-screw, one-6 cylinder Doxford type single-acting two-stroke engine, 15 ¹/₂ knots, by Barclay, Curle & Co of Glasgow. South American service. Sold 1967.

Incorporated as a limited company in 1922, F. T. Everard & Sons Ltd have older origins. Mr Frederick T. Everard was a shipwright who became foreman of a yard building and repairing spritsail barges at Greenhithe in Kent. In 1880 he acquired this yard and, in 1892, went into barge owning with the *Industry*, the first of many Everard spritsail barges. The well known *Cambria* was added to the fleet in 1906. Their first motor vessel was the auxiliary spritsail barge *Grit* built at Greenhithe in 1913. Steam coasters were acquired during the 1914-18 war but the company favoured the motor vessel for dry cargo. They also entered the tanker business with steam and later motor ships, carrying petroleum and edible oils.

Plenty & Son Ltd of Newbury supplied the engines and, in 1932, their works passed to Everard's as the Newbury Diesel Engine Co Ltd. The '-ity' naming started in 1924 with the *Agility* and has become rationalized more recently, with 'S' names for the larger dry cargo, 'C' for the smaller and 'A' for tankers. Family names continued to be used as well.

Ships were built at yards from Greenock to Goole and the company acquired the Fellows & Co Ltd yard at Great Yarmouth and Crabtree's the Great Yarmouth engineers. In the 1950s black hulls gave way to yellow for some ships along with yellow funnels and white replaced the pre-war buff or brown for upperworks. Grey became the hull colour for tankers. Post-war trading included the Baltic and North Africa and, in 1960, the company was involved with a cement carrying enterprise in New Zealand.

There has long been a policy of expansion. J. Wharton of Keadby have been associated since 1952 and Hay's of Glasgow and

Glasgow's Glen & Co joined in 1956 and 1961 respectively. Much modernization came in the 1970s – containers, new ships and, in 1980, the acquisition of Comben Longstaff. Ship management forms an important part of present business in this long standing family company whose flag and funnel pattern have remained unchanged, apart from the use of yellow as well as black.

Full details of the company are in K. S. Garrett's *Everard of Greenhithe*, World Ship Society 1991, and many thanks to Captain Garrett for help with the preparation of pictures and text.

The dry cargo mv *Sagacity* was built in 1946 by the Grangemouth Dockyard; 943 gross tons, 204.5 feet length, single-screw, one 6-cylinder oil engine by Newbury Diesel of Newbury. Sold and broken up in 1972.

The *Angularity*, built in Greenock in 1934, 501 gross tons, 160.5 feet length, single-screw, one 5-cylinder oil engine by Newbury Diesel. Sunk by E-boat in 1941.

The motor tanker *Alacrity*
was built in 1966 by the
Goole Shipbuilding and
Repairing Co.

The dry cargo mv *Seniority* was
built in 1991 by Appledore
Shipbuilders, 3,493 gross tons.

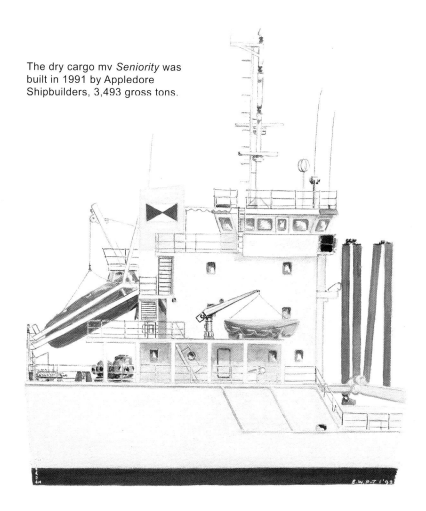

J Fisher & Sons

Today Fisher's of Barrow-in-Furness and their associates are, in the numbers of ships they own, one of the second largest shipping company under the Red Ensign. They date back to 1847 when James Fisher started with sailing vessels and assembled a large fleet, over eighty at its height in the 1870s. These were not only schooners but barques and other rigs in both coastal and deep sea trades, notably ore for the ironworks at Barrow and the products of both the iron and steel enterprises of the town. Fisher's first steamer, the *Sea Fisher*. This was completed in 1883 and, by 1908, the company had eight steam vessels and eighteen sailing craft; the last of these was not sold until 1921.

A decade later the slump pruned the fleet to three, but 1937 saw their first motor vessel, the *Shoal Fisher*, with more following. The *Shoal Fisher* had special long and widened hatches to take gun turrets for the warships fitting out at Barrow, and heavy, awkward cargoes became a Fisher speciality. In 1966 they took delivery of two roll-on, roll-off ships for handling heavy haulage vehicles and their loads and chartered them to the Central Electricity Generating Board for power station work. One was the *Kingsnorth Fisher*, the other the *Aberthaw Fisher* illustrated here. [Both now broken up.]

By the 1960s diversification was the company's strong point, starting with ships chartered out to bring phosphates from Morocco to the Marchon works at Whitehaven. In 1968 a sea-going barge, the *Odin*, was put into service to transfer phosphate cargoes from ships too big to enter Whitehaven and she remained at work there in 1992.

Major advances were the take-over in 1983 of Coe-Metcalf, the Liverpool-based coaster group which specialised in dry cargo work, and, from 1974, the involvement with the carriage of nuclear fuel, first chartering to British Nuclear Fuels Ltd (BNFL) and, from 1979,

also managing the ships owned by BNFL.

The *Pacific Sandpiper* of 1985 is one of their vessels, illustrated here with their present funnel colours which, from 1990, have replaced the Fisher funnel without the 'F'. In 1992, Fisher's own thirty-eight ships were mostly chartered out and they managed a further forty-eight, from Thames passenger catamarans to German heavy lift vessels.

Many thanks to Mr John F. Hornby, Chairman and Managing Director of James Fisher & Sons plc, to the late Mr Derek Blackhurst, the company's historian, to Mr Kevin Routledge, sea-going engineer and modelmaker, and British Nuclear Fuels Ltd.

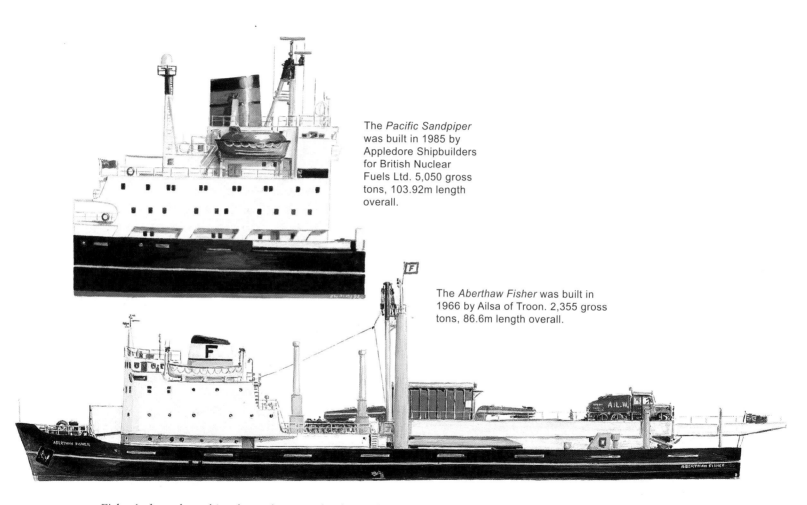

The *Pacific Sandpiper* was built in 1985 by Appledore Shipbuilders for British Nuclear Fuels Ltd. 5,050 gross tons, 103.92m length overall.

The *Aberthaw Fisher* was built in 1966 by Ailsa of Troon. 2,355 gross tons, 86.6m length overall.

Fisher's funnel marking has subsequently changed completely, to a plain blue funnel with 'Fisher' thereon.

Now totally absorbed within the P&O Group, General Steam had a long history. Nicknamed the 'Navvies', the company was founded in 1824, as the houseflag proclaimed (the date was added in 1880), with intentions of a world-wide service; however, the beginnings were modest enough – between London and Margate, but soon extending to Scotland and the near Continental trade within Elbe and Brest limits, although Portugal was soon added. London remained the centre of operations and cattle from the Continent became an important element of the business, starting in 1846 from Rotterdam. The German trade was hampered by the Franco-Prussian War of 1870 but, in 1882, the company entered the Mediterranean with larger ships running to Italy and Sicily. Despite problems with the cattle, the company continued to expand and, in the twentieth century, took over smaller East Coast companies – in 1906 John Crisp & Son in the London, Lowestoft and Norwich trades, in 1919 G. R. Haller of Hull and Leach & Co's London-Ghent services, but not the ships of either of these two concerns. An old association with P&O was cemented in 1920 which allowed General Steam to replace their twenty-three war losses. Fourteen ships were acquired in 1920/1, including five steamers of the distinctive engines-aft design pioneered in 1909. Some ships carried a few passengers.

Parallel with the cargo ships were the summer excursion sailings to the Kent coast, extended to Great Yarmouth and modernised between the wars when the large 'Eagle' paddle steamers were delivered. Continental excursions became possible when, in 1935, the New Medway Steam Packet Company was acquired and motorships built, ending with the *Royal Sovereign* of 1948 (illustrated here) built to replace a war loss of the same name. Cargo ships varied from the 2,385 gross ton *Heron* of 1937 in the Mediterranean trade to the 276 gross ton *Alouette* of 1938. These were motorships, the first had been the *Tern* of 1932 and thereafter few steamers were built. Originally the funnel was plain black but, from 1938, the house flag was placed upon it in some ships and, from 1947, this became more or less standard although in later years there was a reversion to plain black. Most of the cargo ships were named after birds, with animals in the early days, while the excursion ships varied from 'Eagles' to 'Royals' and wore a plain buff funnel, or buff with a black top until, from 1948, the flag was added. Details of the flag seem to have varied. General Steam are no longer ship owners.

Many thanks to Roy Fenton and John Ritchie for help with this company.

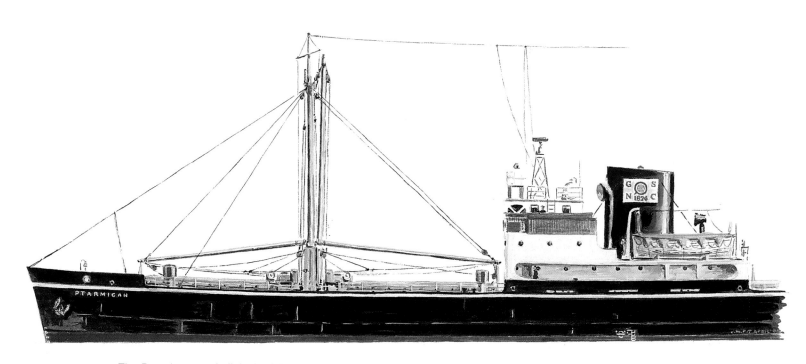

The *Ptarmigan* was built in 1948 by the Grangemouth Dockyard; 959 gross tons; 224.3ft length between perpendiculars.

The *Royal Sovereign* was built in 1948 by William Denny at Dumbarton; 1,851 gross tons; 277.0ft length between perpendiculars.

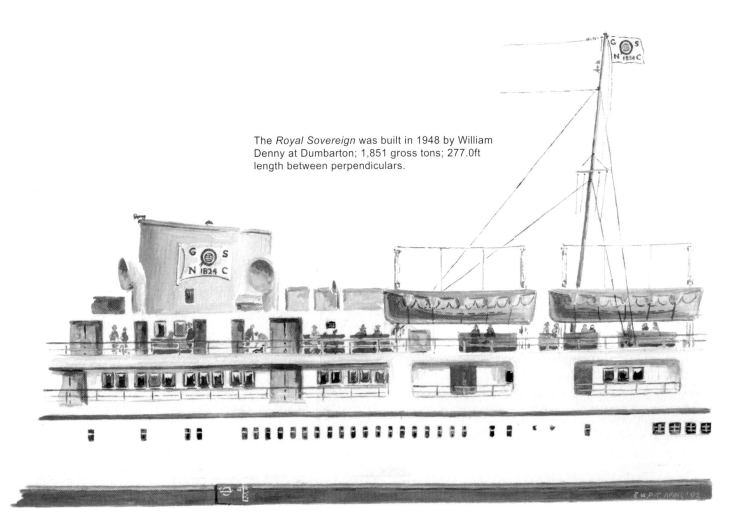

T & J Harrison

For upwards of 140 years T & J Harrison was involved in shipping, modestly in the early days but with increasing investment from the 1860s. The company, which was founded as a family partnership in 1853, remained wholly private. The first ventures were into the wine and particularly brandy trades of the Charente and it was the Charente Steamship Company which was founded in 1871 and expanded in 1884 to own the ships, with Thomas and James Harrison as managers. By this time, however, the partners were looking further afield. Their first steamers were the *Gladiator* and the *Cognac*, both built in 1860, and their sailing ships, from 1863, ran on a regular Indian service, with steamer-operated schedules to the Gulf of Mexico and Brazil soon added. The opening in 1869 of the Suez Canal was a benefit to steam but New Orleans became a major target for Harrison ships, which from 1857 were mostly named after trades and professions, starting with the full-rigged ship *Philosopher*. The last sailing ship was sold in 1889 and the company settled down to steady development on established routes, the Mediterranean, India, the Gulf, Caribbean, Brazil, then from 1902 South Africa. The Rennie Line to Natal was bought in 1911, the ships with the 'In' names, two of which were passenger liners, more 'In'-named passenger ships being added for the South African and West Indies services. Twenty-seven ships were lost during the First World War but in 1917 Rankin, Gilmour of Liverpool was bought, followed in 1920 by the Crown Line of Glasgow and Scrutton's of London. Seven Frederick Leyland ships were acquired in 1933 and four came from Furness Withy two years later. Second World War losses totalled thirty, so from 1947 a big replacement programme was started with the company's first motor ship, the

Herdsman, delivered from Doxfords of Sunderland who built a further twenty-one. A new look came in 1960 with the *Adventurer* and her 180-ton lift Stülcken derrick, and a newer look still in 1973 with the three bulk carriers of the *Wayfarer* Class, with container ships following in 1977. The latter day funnel remained unchanged in colour since 1865, but earlier ones seem to have been plain black. The house flag dates from about 1853.

Many thanks to Duncan Haws for both the history and ship profile.

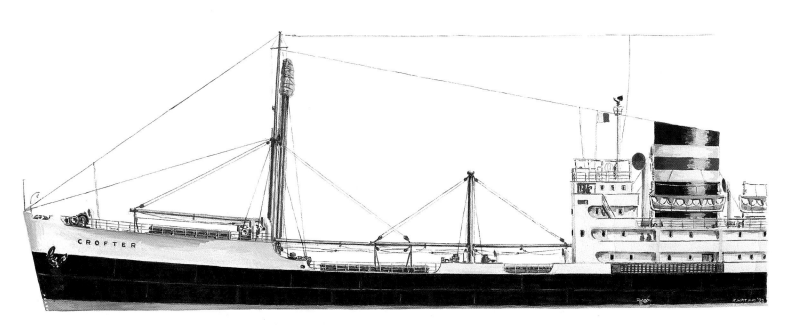

The steamship *Crofter* was built in 1951 by J. Readhead & Sons of South Shields, 8,377 gross tons, 468ft length overall. Single-screw, one triple-expansion reciprocating steam engine and Bauer-Wach low pressure turbine, 12 knots, by the builders. The *Crofter* and *Forester* were the last steamers built for the company and the *Crofter* was the last in service, sold in 1971 and broken up in 1977.

Isle of Man Steam Packet Co.

In business since 1830, the Isle of Man Steam Packet Company must be the oldest of British short sea liner operators. There had been summer steamships services to the island as early as 1819 and winter ones started in 1825, but the Isle of Man needed a company of its own. This gained the mail contract and original sailings between Douglas and Liverpool were soon extended to Glasgow, Dublin and from 1842 to the new port of Fleetwood. Wooden paddle steamers started operations but an iron one appeared with the *Ben-My-Chree* of 1845. The company remained faithful to paddles until the single-screw *Mona* arrived in 1878 followed by two twin-screw vessels, the *Fenella* of 1881 and the *Peveril* of 1884 designed for cargo work in summer and passengers in winter. More destinations were added for the summer services and Ramsey and Peel became additional Manx terminals. The end of the nineteenth century was marked by competition over which the Steam Packet company scored successes with their big paddle steamers, culminating in the *Empress Queen* of 1897. Screw turbine steamers were early on the scene, the *Viking* of 1905 and the *Ben-My-Chree* of 1908; this last, capable of 24 knots, achieved a record Liverpool-Douglas crossing of 2 hours 57 minutes. Purely cargo ships did not appear until 1911 and the company built up their pre-1914 and post-1918 fleet with much secondhand and new tonnage, capped by the centenary ship *Lady of Mann* of 1930. No motor ship was delivered until the cargo vessel *Fenella* arrived in 1951 and the company stayed faithful to the steam turbine with their first car ferries, the *Manx Maid* of 1962 and the *Ben-My-Chree* of 1966. Perhaps the best known of all Steam Packet ships in recent years were the six built by Cammell Laird at Birkenhead between 1946 and 1955, for so many years the mainstay of all services. The last of the class was the *Manxman*, illustrated here, in service until 1982 when she was sold for preservation, albeit in an altered role.

Recent years have been beset by many problems including a renewal of competition, but the company faced the future with a well-founded fleet of motor vessels, designed for vehicle transport, headed by the splendid *King Orry*, illustrated here. She was completed at Genoa in 1975 and was employed in the English Channel as a train ferry until bought in 1990 and given a major refit, but is now no longer in service.

Funnel and house flag have remained the same since 1830 and the Legs of Man badge has always been employed, at first on the paddle boxes, then on stem and stern and on the superstructure of present ships. Although the legs on the Isle of Man flag run clockwise, as do those on the bow badge of the *Manxman* here, the legs on the house flag and modern badge go anti-clockwise. Operates from Heysham and Liverpool.

Many thanks to Richard Kirkman of the Isle of Man Steam Packet Company for his help, and to Russell Plummer.

The *Manxman* was built by Cammel Laird & Co Ltd at Birkenhead in 1955, 2,495 gross tons, 344ft 10in length overall.

The *King Orry* was built by Nuovi Cantieri Liguri, Genoa and completed in 1975 as the train ferry *St Eloi* for Sealink's French subsidiary ALA, and in 1989 was renamed *Channel Entente*, 4,648 gross tons, 119.6 metres length overall. No longer in service.

Among Sweden's premier shipping companies, nowadays concentrating on passenger ships, the Johnson Line is part of the big Axel Johnson trading and industrial group. The original Axel Johnson founded the company in 1873, concentrating on the import of British coal and the export of Swedish matches. Shipping involvement was a natural sequel and in 1890 Rederiaktiebolaget Nordstjernan of Stockholm was established. Early sailings were limited to the Baltic and North Sea, the export of Swedish iron ore becoming a major business, but expansion was rapid. Sailings to the River Plate started in 1904 and into the North and South Pacific from 1914, the latter benefiting from the opening of the Panama Canal. Brazil was added to load coffee, then, later, Central America and much later, in 1948, the Far East.

Motor ships were introduced as early as 1912, the first eight came from Burmeister & Wain at Copenhagen, subsequent motor ships, to which the Johnson Line became wholly committed, mostly from Swedish yards. The country's neutrality in both world wars brought problems, blockade, unrestricted submarine warfare, minefields etc. During the Second World War, Sweden depended for essential supplies on the safe conduct of her ships which had to be painted in the manner illustrated by the *Ecuador*. Both the name and colours were lit up at night. Johnson Line names, incidentally, came from members of the family, members of the Swedish Royal family, and countries and ports served by the ships, also stars and some miscellaneous ones.

Post-1945 Johnson history was a tale of expansion marked, for

example, by the appearance from 1947 of the *Seattle* Class of cargo liner, advanced in design with deck cranes. The 'Rio' Class followed but all were overtaken by the container revolution and the economic problems of the 1970s and '80s which sorely hurt the company.

Salvation has come from participation in the giant Baltic ro-ro ferries and in cruising. All this is described in detail in the company's well-produced centenary history, *The Johnson Line 1890-1990* by Thorsten Rinman, Rinman & Linden AB Gothenburg 1990. There is an English edition to which I am much indebted.

The *Ecuador* (depicted in World War II markings) was built by Götaverken at Gothenburg in 1940; 7,090 gross tons; 420.8 feet length between perpendiculars. Twin-screw, two four-stroke, single-acting, eight-cylinder B&W diesel engines, 17 knots, by Götaverken. South American and Pacific services. She was lost after stranding off the Dutch coast in 1956.

The *Seattle* was built by Kockums at Malmö in 1947; 6,910 gross tons; 478.6 feet length between perpendiculars. Twin-screw, two two-stroke, double-acting, seven-cylinder MAN diesel engines, 20 knots, by Kockums. South American and Pacific services. Sold in 1972.

King Line

This was the first shipping venture of Owen Cosby Phillipps (1863-1937), better known as Lord Kylsant. In 1889 he founded a company to operate a small steamer, the *King Alfred Steamship Co Ltd* (the name of the vessel) but soon altered the title to King Line, with a preference for Welsh kings when further ships were acquired, and Scottish kings for the Scottish Steamship Co subsidiary incorporated in 1896. The colours shown here were the originals, although the buff upperworks were changed to white at an early date. Between 1945 and 1959, however, the buff returned, so the *King Charles* of 1957 must have appeared as illustrated although, after 1959, Clan Line colours prevailed. The black lion rampant with gold collar and chain on the flag appeared on the Philipps' arms.

Tramping, particularly with coal and grain, was the key to the success of the King Line which was associated with the Court Line at one stage, under the elder brother John. While Lord Kylsant went on to establish his shipping empire, management of the King Line passed in 1923 to Dodd, Thomson & Co Ltd of London. Both George Dodd and Sir Vernon Thomson were of exceptional ability, the latter became in 1934 Joint Managing Director of Union Castle and later Chairman. Following Lord Kylsant's propulsion policy for all his ships, motor vessels entered the King Line fleet in 1925. Their first two were built on the corrugated hull principle which did not prove a success. More conventional motor ships followed, indeed the company ordered no further steamers, although steam 'Empire' ships were acquired after the Second World War.

Depression and the collapse of the Kylsant empire in 1931 left the King Line with laid up ships although the motor ships continued in service. Fourteen ships were lost in the Second World War leaving four survivors (1914-18 losses had been five), so new tonnage was

needed. In 1948 the company was taken over by Union Castle and in the 1950s six motor ships were delivered from Harland & Wolff who had built all the Kylsant motor ships. From 1956 King Line was incorporated into British & Commonwealth and Clan funnel colours began to appear. Finally, the company went over to bulk carriers which wore the King Line funnel colours.

Many thanks to John Ritchie and to Alan S. Mallett's history *Idyll of the Kings* (World Ship Society 1980) for help with both drawings and text.

The *King Charles* was built by Harland & Wolff at Belfast in 1957; 5,737 gross tons and 466ft 6in length overall. Single-screw, one four-stroke, single-acting, six-cylinder diesel engine by the builders, 12½ knots. She was sold in 1973 and broken up in 1979.

London & Overseas Freighters

Long established in Mediterranean shipping, the Kulukundis family came to London in 1920 and started a shipping agency under the title of Rethymnis & Kulukundis; Minas Rethymnis was a cousin. The family moved to ownership before the Second World War and, in the 1940s, entered the tramp tanker business, then a novelty. With their cousin Basil Mavroleon they set up in 1948 London & Overseas Freighters to operate both tanker and dry cargo tonnage. A large fleet of motor tankers was created while the dry cargo ships were sold, but company fortunes were dependent on the vagaries of the market. In the 1950s shipyards were so busy that orders were difficult to place, so in 1957 LOF took an interest in the Sunderland yard of Austin & Pickersgill which they were able to secure completely in 1970 along with Bartrams of Sunderland. Both built SD14s, which were sold world-wide and the *London Cavalier* illustrated here is a good example.

Subsidiary companies were created, some registered in Bermuda; London & Overseas Tankers in 1956, London & Overseas Bulk Carriers in 1960. In 1961 LOF joined with the Gibbs family of South Wales to start Welsh Ore Carriers. The 1970s and 1980s, however, were decades of acute difficulty for shipowners and much had to be pruned. In 1993, the fleet under the Red Ensign comprised two sister 61,000-ton deadweight tankers, the *London Spirit* and the *London Victory*, the 150,000-ton deadweight tanker, the *London Pride* and the *London Enterprise*.

From the start of LOF in 1948, ships' names were given the prefix 'London' and the right to display the coat of arms of the City of London on the bridge front (2). The flags are (1) London & Overseas Freighters, (3) London & Overseas Bulk Carriers and (4) Welsh Ore Carriers. This last had a red, black-topped funnel with the same device as the flag, while that of London & Overseas Bulk Carriers had a variant to LOF, yellow with the red star on a white band edged by a thin blue band at top and bottom.

1

2

DOMINE DIRIGE NOS

Many thanks to M. Kinnaird and Jonathan Johnson of London & Overseas Freighters, to Roy Fenton, N. R. Pugh and John Ritchie for their help in preparing this set. Following their 1977 history of LOF the World Ship Society have now produced a later one to which I am grateful for the details of the ships.

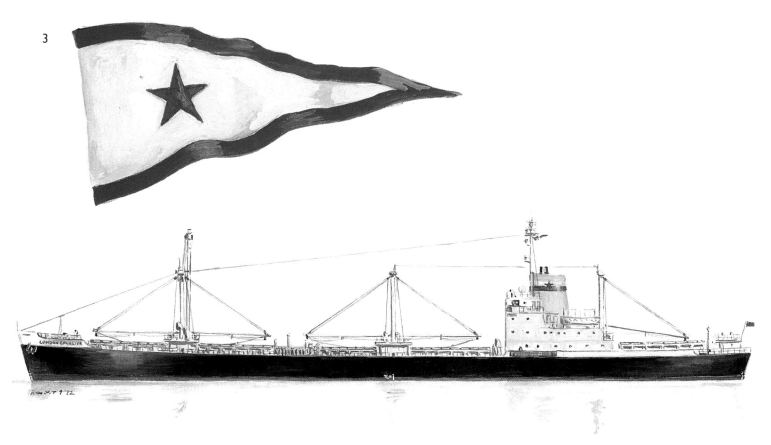

3

The *London Cavalier*, an SD14, was built by Austin & Pickersgill at Sunderland in 1972, 9,210 gross tons, 140.9 metres in length overall. Single-screw, one two-stroke single-acting Sulzer-type five-cylinder diesel engine by Hawthorn, Leslie of Newcastle, 14.5 knots. She was sold in 1980.

4

The *London Victory* was built by Mitsui Engineering & Shipbuilding, Ichihara, Japan, in 1982, 36,865 gross tons, 219 metres in length overall. Single-screw, one Burmeister & Wain two-stroke single-acting seven-cylinder diesel engine built under licence by Mitsui at Tamano, 15.5 knots.

A. P. Møller-Maersk Line

With over 100 ships from bulk carriers to anchor handling tugs, A. P. Møller of Copenhagen must be one of the world's largest shipping companies. They started modestly in 1904 when the Steamship Company Svendborg was founded by Captain Peter Maersk Møller and his son Arnold Peter, although Captain Møller had owned a steamer from 1886, the first to carry the seven-pointed star on a blue band round the funnel, which distinguishes the fleet today. From 1906 it became customary to name ships after the family using the family name Maersk as a suffix, although nowadays as a prefix too, and the first 'Maersk' ship was the *Peter Maersk* of that year. Another company was created, the Steamship Company of 1912, and in 1917-18 A. P. Møller founded the Odense Steel Shipyard which, in 1921, delivered the first motor ship to the fleet. Oil tankers were introduced in 1928 and between the wars the company became well established in the liner trade between the USA and the Far East.

World War II losses were heavy but new building was rapid, with fast dry cargo ships ordered and, from 1961, bulk carriers. In 1963 a new shipyard was added at Lindø near Odense, large enough to build the size of ship now required, including the 339,000 tons deadweight VLCC *Kristine Maersk*. Diversification increased from the 1960s, refrigerated ships, container ships, petroleum products carriers, gas carriers, supply ships for the oil platforms, along with anchor handling tugs, ro-ro ships and car carriers.

Ships fly the Danish ensign, with some under the Red Ensign too. All have the bright blue hull, matching the blue of the flag and funnel, which replaced the grey from 1955. Originally ships had the usual black hull, but grey was introduced in 1923 and became standard from 1934. It had been the practice from an early date, certainly from 1920, to paint the name of the ship on the side of the hull, but this has now been dropped in favour of Maersk Line which is carried by the container ships, harking back to the use of this title for the USA-Far East liner service started in 1928.

Many thanks to Roy Fenton in the UK, to Søren Thorsøe in Denmark, and to Palle Genckel of A. P. Møller in Copenhagen for their great help in the preparation of this set of colours.

The *Hans Maersk* was built in 1916 by A. Vuijke & Zonen in Holland, 1,999 gross tons, 292.7 feet length overall.

The *Herta Maersk* was built in 1948 by Burmeister & Wain, Copenhagen, 4,325 gross tons, 359.5 feet length overall.

The *Peter Maersk* was built in 1949 by Eriksbergs M V at Gothenburg, 8,805 gross tons, 478.8 feet length overall.

The container ship *Mette Maersk* was built in 1989 by the Odense Steel Shipyard at Lindø, 60,000 tons deadweight with a capacity of over 4,000 TEUs, 294 metres length overall.

Nourse Line

James Nourse was a master mariner who turned to shipowning when he ordered the 839-ton iron full-rigged ship *Ganges* launched in 1861, setting the tradition for river names: Indian, Irish, English and Scottish, European, settling for Indian only when the steamers came. In 1864 Captain Nourse contracted with the Crown Agents for the Colonies to carry indentured labour between India and the West Indies. This was the coolie traffic in which the Nourse Line achieved eminence, undertaking in addition passages to Mauritius and Fiji. Sailing ships were ordered new and acquired secondhand, all iron or steel, the last being built in 1894. Nourse had no steamers apart from a tug at Calcutta until 1904 when the striking funnel design symbolizing Neptune's crown appeared. The sailing ships remained until 1910; four years later not only was there a war but the outward coolie trade ended.

First World War losses were limited to two ships, yet the company felt in a weak position with the need to find a new business and were glad in 1917 to accept an offer from P&O. Rice and gunny sacks were now the main cargoes, more steamers were built and in 1939 the first motor ship, the *Bhima*. Second World War losses were heavy with only three ships left in 1945, so a considerable motor ship building programme followed. Traditional trades were, however, in decline so the ships were put on tramping or charter to other members of the P&O Group. In the early 1960s tankers were allocated to the Nourse flag which received its last dry cargo ship in 1962, but from 1964 the main P&O tramping concern, the Hain S.S. Co Ltd, merged with the Nourse Line as Hain-Nourse

Management. The following year the Nourse Line was taken over completely under the title of Hain-Nourse Ltd with a new funnel and flag and a dark blue hull. (Not shown here.)

Preparation of this set has been dependent on John Ritchie and on the history of the Nourse Line by F. W. Perry and W.A. Laxon, published by the World Ship Society in 1991. Many thanks.

The full rigged steel ship *Mersey* was built by Charles Connell, Glasgow, in 1894, 1,829 gross tons, 270.7 feet length between perpendiculars.

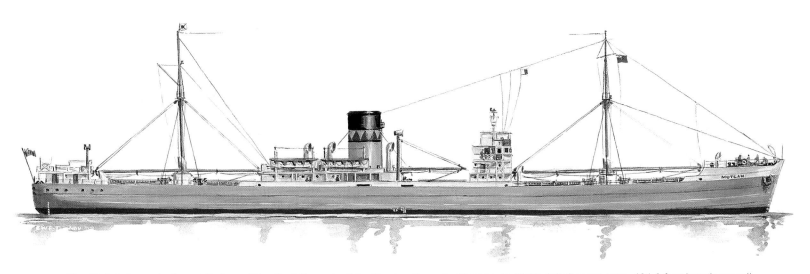

The *Mutlah* (named after a tributary of the Hughli) was built by Charles Connell, Glasgow, in 1947, 6,652 gross tons, 431.8 feet length overall.

Osborn & Wallis

William Osborn of Bristol and Humphrey Wallis of Cardiff combined to form a steamship company in the 1890s. Wallis was a coal exporter and Osborn an importer, so coal became and remained central to O&W operations as merchants and shippers. Their early steamers were tramps, mainly in the Spanish trade, coal out from Cardiff, copper pyrites in from Huelva for the United Alkali works at Netham, Bristol. *The Stakesby*, illustrated here, was one of seven, all acquired secondhand and these were the ships which wore the OW monogram on their black funnels.

At the same time Osborn & Wallis were developing a local coal trade. They had Severn trows, steam barges and steam coastal colliers. Coal was carried well up the Avon to riverside works, for the barges were able to pass under the bridges, while the coastal colliers supplied the power station at Portishead, opened in 1929. Vintage ships stayed a long time with Osborn & Wallis, but one new building was the *Druid Stoke*, delivered by Charles Hill of Bristol in 1929. The *Rockleaze*, illustrated here, was however secondhand, built in 1924 and bought by O&W in 1939 from the Ald Shipping Company, along with the *Downleaze*. The first Osborn & Wallis motor ship came in 1940 and their final tonnage was delivered new by Charles Hill, the motor vessel *Colston* in 1955, her sister *Brandon* in 1957. These ships carried an orangey-red funnel. Shipping services ceased in 1970 with the sale of the last three vessels.

R. M. Parsons of Bristol compiled the Osborn & Wallis story in the October 1986 issue of *Ships Monthly*, to which I am indebted, while Fred J. Greenham, John Ritchie and former Editor Robert Shopland supplied much detail, to all of whom many thanks.

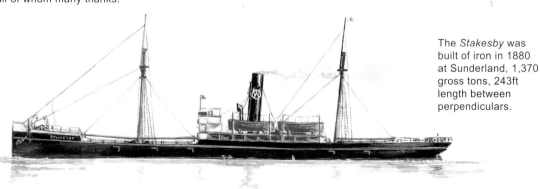

The *Stakesby* was built of iron in 1880 at Sunderland, 1,370 gross tons, 243ft length between perpendiculars.

The *Rockleaze* was built by the Goole Shipbuilding & Repairing Company in 1924 as the *Glynconwy*; 486 gross tons, 156ft 2ins length between perpendiculars.

The *Brandon* was built by Charles Hill at Bristol in 1957; 586 gross tons, 169ft 9ins length overall.

Palm Line

This company was formed in 1949 to take over the deep-sea ships of the Unilever organisation. Lever Brothers had entered shipping in 1916 when they bought the eight steamers of H. Watson & Co of Manchester and formed them into the Bromport Steamship Co (1), derived from Bromborough Port, to provide the link between their Merseyside and West African interests. Their second shipping acquisition was the Niger Company (2) in 1920, originally a chartered company founded in 1886 as the Royal Niger Company with their own ensign (3). In 1923 the Bromport ships were sold and in 1929 the Niger Company merged with their rivals, acquired by Levers that same year, the African & Eastern Trade Corporation (4), a 1919 amalgamation of four firms. They had entered shipowning in 1923 and introduced the 'ian' suffix names. The merger was named the United Africa Company (5) operating both deep-sea ships and river and coastal craft. UAC had two houseflags, the first (5) from 1929 to 1936, the second (6) from 1936 to 1949 for their ships and until 1973 in West Africa when UAC International was founded with a new flag.

Palm Line took over fifteen ships, of which the *Conakrian* is a good example, renaming them with a 'Palm' suffix; she became the *Dahomey Palm*. UAC had modernised their fleet during the 1930s, ordering ships from British and German yards, for Unilever had heavy investments in Germany. Second World War losses were considerable but fresh tonnage followed. Under Palm Line the ships became common carriers and not limited to Unilever business. In 1950 they were admitted to the West African Lines Conference. Palm Line continued the building programme with dry cargo ships and vegetable oil tankers, indeed the fleet

was replaced and in 1961 stood at a maximum of twenty-four, the year the *Lagos Palm* was delivered.

Emergence of national shipping companies in West Africa, political problems, port congestion and the advent of containers led to reductions in the Palm Line fleet and eventual disposal of the last ships by 1989.

Many thanks to Roy Fenton and John Ritchie for helping with this set, the flags particularly demanded much research.

1

3

2

4

5

6

The *Conakrian* was built by the Furness Shipbuilding Company at Haverton Hill-on-Tees in 1937 for the United Africa Company, 4,876 gross tons, 438.3 feet length overall.

The *Lagos Palm* was built by Swan Hunter & Wigham Richardson at Newcastle in 1961, 5,927 gross tons, 473.6 feet length overall.

Queenship Navigation

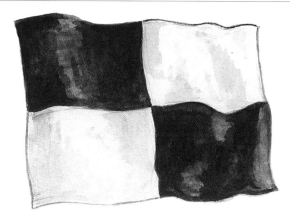

Few shipping companies begin with the letter 'Q' and Queenship Navigation was really an offshoot of Cheeswright & Ford's London & Channel Islands Steamship Co Ltd, founded in 1899. Their ships were named with a 'Queen' suffix and their flag (top) was quartered blue and white. In 1936 they sold out to Coast Lines and the following year the company name was changed to British Channel Islands Shipping Co Ltd, with the same flag but a different funnel, buff, white over blue bands, black top; after 1945 this changed to buff, blue band, black top.

Cheeswright & Ford had an associated tramp concern, formed in 1934, Merchants Line, which also passed to Coast Lines. In 1943 this was reconstituted as British Channel Traders Ltd and in 1947 renamed Queenship Navigation Ltd. British Channel Traders and Queenship had, it seems, the same funnel and the blue saltire and red Q flag was introduced before 1947. To explain the Queenship parentage I have drawn the Cheeswright & Ford flag and given the *Tudor Queen* the British Channel Islands post-1945 funnel she would have worn for about a year, for in 1946 she was transferred to Queenship. In 1965 Queenship's last three ships passed to Britain Steamship Co Ltd with Comben Longstaff & Co Ltd as managers.

Many thanks to Roy Fenton and to Captain K.S. Garrett for their assistance with this set and to Douglas Chesterton whose fleet list I have used, while the *Tudor Queen* is inspired by a Laurence Dunn cut-away drawing.

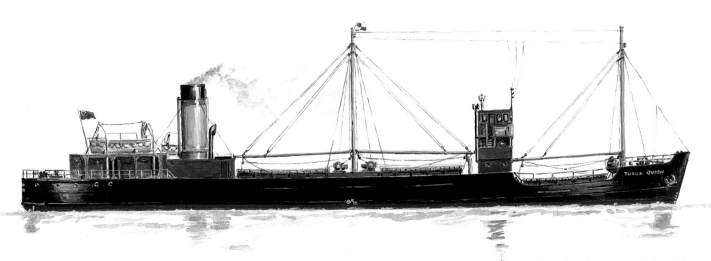

The *Tudor Queen*, the prototype of many war-built coasters, was built by the Burntisland Shipbuilding Co on the Forth in 1941 for the British Channel Islands Shipping Co Ltd, 1,029 gross tons, 212 feet 4 inches length overall. Single-screw, one triple expansion reciprocating engine by David Rowan of Glasgow. Sold in 1946 to Queenship Navigation and in 1959 to Coast Lines, Liverpool, and broken up in that year.

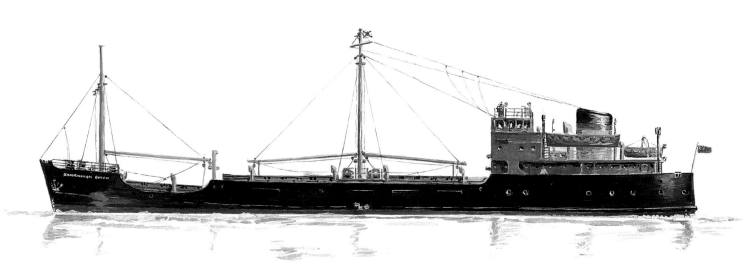

The *Sandringham Queen* was built by the Goole Shipbuilding & Engineering Co Ltd in 1955, 1,308 gross tons, 232 feet 8 inches length overall. Single-screw, one two-stroke single-acting seven-cylinder British Polar oil engine, Glasgow. Sold in 1965 to the Britain Steamship Co Ltd.

Ropner's

Founded in 1874, the company began modestly when Robert Ropner forsook a partnership and established himself as a steamship owner and coal exporter based on West Hartlepool. The red and white quartered house flag and funnel mark on a black funnel were used from the start, the colours of the arms of the City of Magdeburg, Robert Ropner's birthplace. Fleet expansion was rapid, encouraged by participation in the South Wales coal trade. From 1887 steel ships were being ordered and in the following year Robert Ropner bought a shipyard at Stockton-on-Tees which remained in business until 1925. In the 1880s the use of the 'by' suffix became standard naming practice, selected from towns and villages, many local like *Lackenby* although the *Trunkby* of 1896 was the first of twenty-two trunk-decked ships (not the same as turret deck), whose method of construction gave greater stability.

The complexity of owning ships on the 64th shares system encouraged Sir Robert Ropner (he was knighted in 1902) to found in 1903 a limited company, the Pool Shipping Co Ltd, with R. Ropner & Co as managers. The 'pool' suffix joined the 'by' as an acknowledged Ropner naming style. Larger ships with capacious bunkers were now being ordered for the company's world-wide tramping operations, but World War I brought heavy losses, twenty-eight ships in all, although Ropner's hit back, sinking one U-boat and damaging another. In 1915 the company became limited liability and a further reorganisation followed in 1919. The house flag continued to bear the initials RR & Co although in the early 1950s these were replaced by the family coat of arms as illustrated here.

Dark grey had long been the colour of Ropner hulls, with the ship's name in large letters on the side amidships a distinctive feature, certainly present from the 1900s. The bottle green for hull and

funnel did not come until 1946. Astute management guided the Ropner fleet between the wars, with much new tonnage completed during the Depression when prices were low, many ships coming from William Gray of West Hartlepool. World War II losses were heavy, thirty-three ships by enemy action and three strandings; only eleven remained in 1945. But again 'Ropner's Navy' retaliated and disabled two U-boats which were subsequently sunk.

Post-war developments included the founding in 1946 of the Ropner or Gulf Line to run between Europe and the Gulf of Mexico.

By this time Ropner's were using motor ships, the first had appeared in 1936, but the Doxford-engined *Daleby* of 1950 (illustrated) set a new standard; she and her sister *Deerpool* could carry twelve passengers. The Gulf Line ceased trading in 1956 by which time the company had entered the tanker business. Since 1948 they have been a public company, Ropner plc, and during the 1960s commenced a diversification programme with engineering, insurance broking and property divisions. Ships remained the core of the family business and in 1993, two, the *Otterpool* (illustrated) and the *Oakby*, were owned and operated by Ropner's, and five were managed for British Steel plc, one of these being on bareboat charter to British Steel but owned by Ropner's.

Much help has been given to this feature by Mr P. S. Robinson of Ropner Shipping Services Ltd with the approval of the Chairman Mr Jeremy Ropner, and I must thank too my colleague John Ritchie.

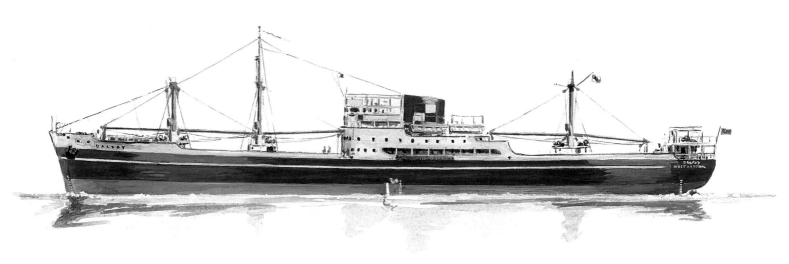

The *Daleby* was built by Sir James Laing & Sons Ltd, Sunderland in 1950, 5,171 gross tons, 445 feet 2 inches length overall.

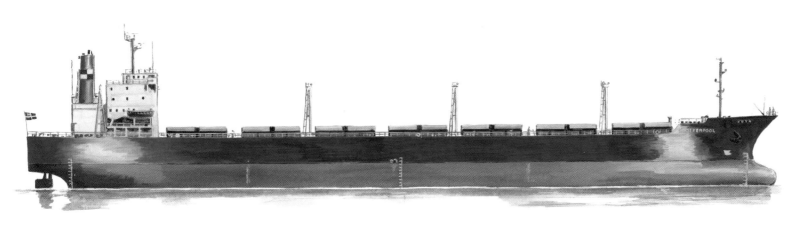

The *Otterpool* was built by Hitachi Zosen, Innoshima Works, Hiroshima, Japan, in 1982 and acquired by the Ropner Shipping Company in 1990, 64,592 metric tonnes deadweight, 225.00 metres length overall. Now scrapped

Shell Tankers

Founded in 1892 when the *Murex* was launched, the tanker fleet has grown from such pioneers as the *Conch* of 5,000 tons deadweight to the 69,500 tons deadweight *Zidona* almost a century later (1989) via such as the *Helix*, 17,780 tons deadweight, VLCCs, gas carriers and much else. From 1892 to 1907 the company house flag (2) bore the initials of the two Samuel brothers, the founders, trading under the title of M. Samuel & Co, originally importers of exotic shells to adorn trinket boxes. But their oil business grew fast with production centred on the Dutch East Indies to the extent that in 1907 Shell amalgamated with Royal Dutch and created Anglo Saxon Petroleum to run the ships. For this, house flag (3) was chosen, an obvious descendant of (2) and the ships continued to be named after sea shells as they are today. Flag (3) remained until 1945 but from 1932 flag (4) was in use and stayed until 1963 when it was modernised to flag (5), slightly modified in 1972 but altered again in 1973 to the present flag (1).

Funnels have undergone similar changes, from the use of the house flag on the side as in the *Conch* with the letters SS & Co added after 1897, to the buff with a black top from 1907 to 1945, to the red shell added from the latter year as shown in the *Helix*, to the 1963 transposal of colours which remains today, although the shell has been simplified from 1972/3 in line with the flag.

All this is described in detail by Stephen Howarth in his Shell history *Sea Shell*, Thomas Reed 1992 and by J. L. Loughran in *Mercantile House Flags and Funnels*, Waine Research 1979. I am indebted to both and to John Ritchie for providing ship details.

2

3

4

5

The *Helix* was built by Swan Hunter & Wigham Richardson, Newcastle upon Tyne in 1953, 12,089 gross tons, 555 feet length overall.

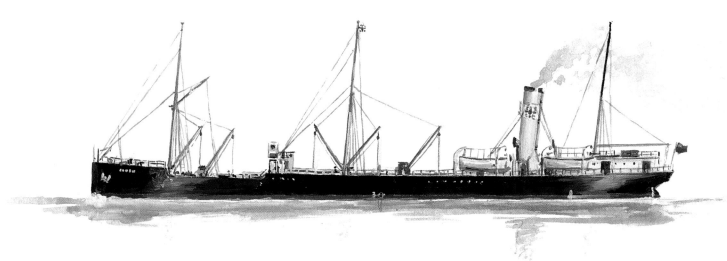

The *Conch* was built by William Gray at West Hartlepool in 1892, 3,555 gross tons, 338 feet length overall.

The *Zidona* was built by Burmeister & Wain, Copenhagen in 1989, 43,398 gross tons, 751 feet length overall (Panamax dimensions).

W J Tatem

William James Tatem, born in 1868, came from Appledore in North Devon. After a brief time at sea, he joined in 1886 a Cardiff shipping company as a clerk. Eleven years later he was confident enough to enter shipowning on his own account with the newly-built *Lady Lewis*, a tramp steamer which brought him large and rapid profits. More new ships soon followed, each owned by a single ship company but all managed by W. J. Tatem & Co and for the most part named after West Country towns, villages and rivers. In the 1900s, with Welsh steam coal in universal demand, Cardiff was the energy capital of the world and large fleets were built up for the export trade. W. J. Tatem's became the largest by 1905, the year two turret steamers were ordered from Doxford's of Sunderland, the *Wellington* and *Torrington* (illustrated), at 5,600 gross tons the biggest ships to be registered at Cardiff at that time.

Nine ships were lost during the 1914-18 War, five sold and six added. In 1916 Tatem remodelled his company with the creation of the Atlantic Shipping and Trading Company, which had a London office. At the same time the registry of the ships was changed from Cardiff to London. At the end of the war Baron Glanely of St Fagans, as he became in 1918, sold his whole fleet at great profit but replaced them with six new ships. The difficult years between the wars were weathered because the company had a diversity of interests, at one point all save one ship were laid up. Like other Welsh owners, W. J. Tatem had a hand in blockade running during the Spanish Civil War and in 1938 the company's first motor ship, the *Lady Glanely*, was delivered although steamers continued to be built. Eight ships were lost (one by stranding) during the Second World War and in 1942 Lord Glanely was killed in an air raid on Weston-super-Mare.

He had become known for his horses at Newmarket as much as for his ships. Four vessels survived the war, now under the management of his nephew G. C. Gibson who embarked on a post-war rebuilding programme which included the steam reciprocating and turbine powered *Lord Glanely* (illustrated). Motor ships had, however, come to stay; the last was delivered in 1965, but prospects were dim in the long distance tramping trades and in 1973 Tatem's withdrew from shipping.

All this is based on P. M. Heaton's book *Tatem's of Cardiff* published in 1987, a sequel to his and Harold Appleyard's *The Baron Glanely of St Fagans and W. J. Tatem Ltd*, of 1980.

The *Torrington*, a turret deck steamer, was built by William Doxford, Sunderland, in 1905, 5,597 gross tons, 390.3 feet length between perpendiculars. Single-screw, triple-expansion reciprocating steam engine. Torpedoed 1917.

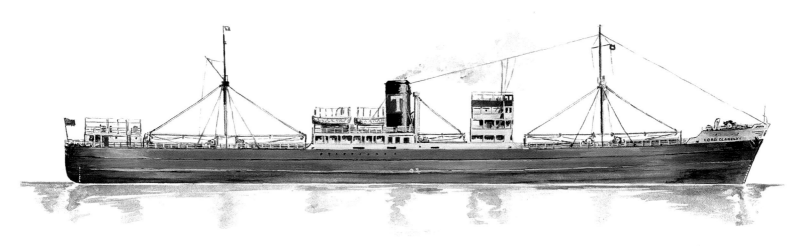

The *Lord Glanely* was built by William Pickersgill and Sons, Sunderland, in 1947, 5,640 gross tons, 450.7 feet length overall. Single-screw, triple expansion reciprocating steam engine and low pressure turbine by North Eastern Marine Engineering, Sunderland. Sold 1960 and broken up 1973.

Union-Castle

One of Britain's more distinctive shipping companies whose shade of lavender is hard for the artist to achieve, Union-Castle was an amalgamation in 1900 of two established lines in the South African service, the Union Steam Ship Company Ltd founded in 1853 which in 1857 gained the mail contract to the Cape, and Donald Currie's Castle Line which in 1876 secured a share in this contract. The two companies tried to outdo each other in the size and speed of their ships, with the Union Line tending to outclass the Castle. When in 1899 the Cape government insisted on a unified mail contract, amalgamation was the solution, achieved early the following year. The new houseflag (1) was an attractive combination of the Union Line (2) and the Castle Line (3), while the Union-Castle funnel perpetuated the Castle one (the Union funnel had latterly been plain buff). The lavender hull was also inherited from the Castle Line whose ships had varied from light grey to slate, while Union hulls had been white.

Acquired by Lord Kylsant's Royal Mail Group in 1912, Union-Castle survived the collapse of this empire in 1931 and by 1939 had achieved under, Sir Vernon Thomson, an impressive modernisation programme which included the building of the refrigerated *Rochester Castle* (illustrated) in 1937 and the 1938 refit of the 1930-built *Winchester Castle* (illustrated). In 1956 Union-Castle joined the Clan Line to form the British & Commonwealth Shipping Company whose burgee (4) was flown in conjunction with the Union-Castle houseflag, the new design a merger of the Clan lion and Union-Castle saltire.

Many thanks to Duncan Haws for advice on this set and to the book, *The Cape Run* by W. H. Mitchell and L. A. Sawyer with drawings by Nigel V. Robinson (Terence Dalton 1984).

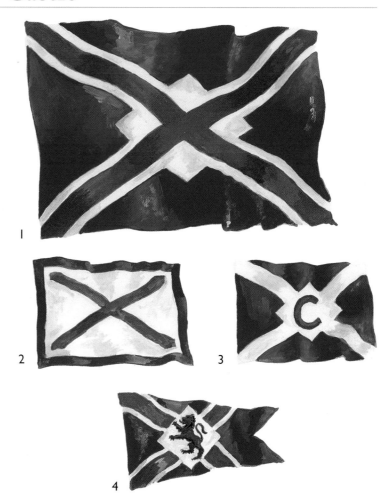

1

2

3

4

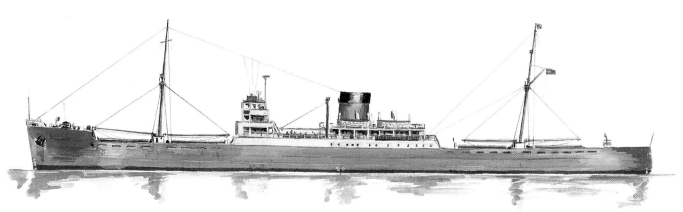

The *Rochester Castle* was built by Harland & Wolff, Belfast in 1937, 7,795 gross tons, 474.2 feet length overall. Single-screw, one two-stroke double-acting eight-cylinder diesel engine by the builders. Speed 16 knots. She was the lead ship of the 'Pedestal' Convoy, which in August 1942 raised the siege of Malta. Sold in 1970, she sailed under the Chinese flag until 1983.

The *Winchester Castle* was built by Harland & Wolff, Belfast in 1930 with two funnels but rebuilt in 1938 as illustrated, 20,001 gross tons, 657 feet length overall. Twin-screw, a pair of two-stroke double-acting ten-cylinder diesel engines by the builders. Speed 20 knots. Broken up in 1960.

Steamer services up the Norwegian coast started as early as 1828 under private initiative, shakily at first, but from 1838 with government backing and more success. In 1851 the Bergen Steamship Company was founded and secured a mail contract, followed in 1857 by Trondheim's Nordenfjelske Company with their *Haakon Jarl*. Both concerns started joint sailings to Hammerfest from 1865 and the government withdrew their services. Tourism became an important element from the early 1870s but in the north it was felt that local interests were being neglected. The solution was found by Captain Richard With of Tromsø who in 1881, with local capital, founded the Vesteraalens Steamship Company, starting with the second-hand steamer *Vesteraalen* of 1865, 220 gross tons, which remained afloat for 106 years. Bigger ships followed, along with proposals for a coastal express service backed by the state. In 1893, the hurtigruten (coastal express) was born with the *Vesteraalen* of 1891 taking the first sailing from Trondheim to Hammerfest. Soon the Bergenske and Nordenfjelske companies joined in and from 1898 the hurtigruten was extended southwards to Bergen and northwards round the North Cape to Vadsø, lengthened in 1908 to Kirkenes near the Russian border.

Both World Wars provided problems, shortage of coal and, in the Second, attacks by Allied aircraft and submarines. Post-1945 services have developed into nightly departures all the year from Bergen for the eleven-day round trip, using at first pre-war ships like the *Lofoten* (illustrated) and then motor vessels, traditional at first but from the 1960s of more revolutionary design like the *Lofoten* (illustrated); then from the 1980s vessels with side loading facilities. Control of the hurtigruten has shifted to the north with Vesteraalens merged with the Narvik company Ofotens as Ofotens og Vesteraalens Dampskibsselskab. Right, the later version of the Vesteraalens houseflag is the Norwegian postal ensign, authorised in 1898 and flown by the express ships.

For details of the ships and their history see *Coastal Express* by Mike Bent, Conway Maritime Press, 1987, a work to which I am indebted, as indeed I am to the company Ofotens og Vesteraalens Dampskibsselskab.

The ss *Lofoten* was built by Fredrikstad M/V, Fredrikstad in 1932, 1,576 gross tons, 248.6 feet length overall. Single-screw, triple-expansion reciprocating steam engine. Sold in 1964 to Cypriot owners but lost by fire in 1966.

The mv *Lofoten* was built by Akers M/V, Oslo in 1964, 2,597 gross tons, 286.8 feet length overall. Single-screw, one two-stroke single-acting seven- cylinder Burmeister & Wain diesel engine by Akers M/V. Speed 16.75 knots.

Williamstown

Readers may be puzzled by this subject, but Williamstown Shipping was a subsidiary, incorporated in 1937, of Comben Longstaff & Co Ltd, the well-known London-based collier owners serving South Coast power stations. The first Williamstown ship was a motor vessel, built in Holland in 1937 and named the *Williamstown*, possibly in deference to William Longstaff. She is believed to have worn the Comben Longstaff flag and funnel of the day which came in two versions, an earlier intertwined CL on flag and funnel (2) and a later simplified design (3) which could have been introduced in about 1935. The intertwined version has affinities with the intertwined RL of Richards, Longstaff, from whom Comben Longstaff broke away in 1934. One Williamstown ship, the *Worthtown* of 1939, was sunk at Dunkirk, salvaged by the Germans but recaptured in 1945 to become the *Empire Worthtown* and then the *Glamorganbrook*. But she sank the following year.

Most Comben Longstaff new buildings after the war were put under Williamstown ownership but Comben Longstaff management, wearing the contemporary CL funnel and flag (1). They included the coal-burning *Londonbrook* (illustrated) of the 'L' Class and the motor *Chesterbrook* (illustrated) of the 'C' Class. Williamstown ceased to own ships from 1967 but stayed a dormant company until bought by F. T. Everard & Sons Ltd in 1980.

I am indebted to Captain K. S. Garrett for the details of this set and to Louis Loughran whose houseflag research is monumental.

2

3

The *Londonbrook* was built by John Lewis of Aberdeen in 1946, 960 gross tons, 218.5 feet length overall. Single-screw, triple expansion reciprocating steam engine by the builders. Sold in 1963 to Willie's of Cardiff and, in 1966, to Greek interests.

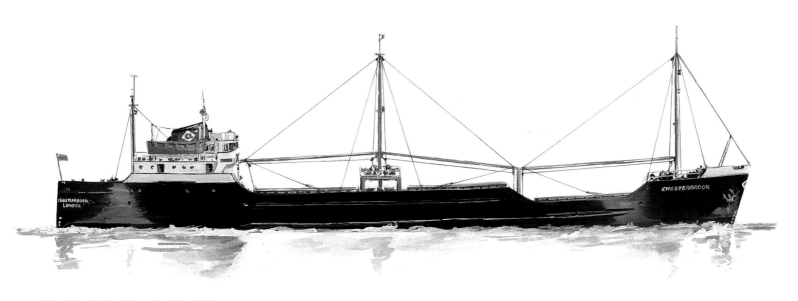

The *Chesterbrook* was built by Clelands' of Wallsend in 1963, 1,594 gross tons, 265 feet 8 inches length overall. Single-screw, one four-stroke single-acting six-cylinder Klockner, Humboldt, Deutz of Cologne diesel engine. Sold in 1976 to Greek interests and scrapped in 1985.

Chandris (Candris)

John D. Chandris came from the Aegean island of Chios. After serving under another Greek owner, Chandris set up on his own account in 1915 with the sailing ship *Dimitrios*, which was followed in 1919 by two steamers, the *Dimitrios* and the *Vlassios*, both small but soon replaced by bigger vessels. A passenger ship for coastal work was acquired in 1922 and it was not long before Chandris was into world-wide tramping and tankers. A London office opened not long before the Second World War, at the time cruising started with the *Patris*, acquired in 1936 and registered under the Red Ensign.

Second World War losses numbered four, but after 1945 expansion continued into the emigrant trade, handled by the London-based Charlton Steam Shipping Company. There was now no stopping the growth of a shipping empire, VLCCs, a passenger service to Australia and more cruising. Much tonnage was secondhand, the United States Lines *America* became the *Australis*, the Union-Castle *Kenya Castle* the *Amerikanis* (illustrated), converted at the company's own yard at Perama outside Piraeus. The first new cruising liner was the *Horizon* (illustrated) built in 1990 at Papenburg on the Ems. She has been followed by the *Zenith*, built in 1992, while the *Meridian* was the former Italian *Galileo Galilei*. Chandris also entered the short-sea cruising business with such ships as the *Carina*, formerly the Isle of Man Steam Packet Company's *Mona's Queen* of 1946, and the *Fantasia*, formerly the Heysham-Belfast passenger ship *Duke of York*, which also operated on the Harwich-Hook service. The Chandris Group prospers, not only with ships, but hotel interests, as well as shipbroking, insurance and agency work. Aquired by Royal Caribbean International in 1997, the ships still carry the same funnel colours.

Many thanks to Duncan Haws and John Ritchie for help with this set.

The Amerikanis (American Lady) was built by Harland & Wolff, Belfast in 1952 as the *Kenya Castle* for Union-Castle, 17,041 gross tons, 576 feet 6 inches length overall. Twin-screw, double reduction geared turbines. Speed 17½ knots. Sold to the Chandris group in 1967 and converted for cruising.

The Horizon was built by Meyer Werft, Papenburg, Germany in 1990, 46,811 gross tons, 207.59 metres length overall. Twin-screw, controllable pitch, four MAN/B&W diesel engines driving two double reduction gearboxes. Speed 21.40 knots. Transferred to Island Cruises in 2005.

Yeoward Line

Richard and Lewis Yeoward established a fruit importing business in Liverpool in 1894, their main supplies coming from the Canary Islands, Spain and Portugal. Using chartered tonnage at first, in 1900 they moved into shipowning by buying tonnage from the Cork Steamship Company. But in 1903 they started to build their own ships, going to the Caledon yard at Dundee, who had delivered the Cork SS ships they already had. While the Cork ships bore bird names in English, the Yeoward Brothers chose bird names in Spanish beginning with 'A' and at a later date ending in 'A' too, *Aguila*, Eagle; *Alondra*, Lark; *Alca*, Razorbill. The flag and funnel colours carried the red and gold of Spain and the Yeoward ships could be distinguished by their three masts and split superstructure. Their silhouettes did not alter from the *Ardeola* of 1904 to the *Alca* of 1927 (illustrated) although size increased, as did passenger complement, from the twelve cabins of the above *Ardeola* to the over forty of the later ships. They became very popular.

Neither of the World Wars were kind to the Yeoward Line. In the First they lost five ships and in the Second three, leaving by 1945 only the *Alca*. Two other ships had been sold during the Depression for service on the Chilean coast and, although there were plans in 1938 for newbuilding, a joint service with MacAndrews was begun instead. The *Alca* survived until 1954 when she was chartered out and then in 1955 she was broken up. Yeowards themselves now reverted to chartering until in 1959 the Aznar Line of Bilbao took

over their services with Yeoward's acting as agents. The company continue in a diversified role: travel, road haulage and distribution have been their interests as well as fruit.

David Burrell has provided all the historical details which have also been recorded in *Sea Breezes* (May 1969) in an article by Craig J. M. Carter and in *Ships Monthly* (March 1988) in an article on the *Alca* by Malcolm Fimister.

The *Alca* was built by Caledon of Dundee in 1927, 3,590 gross tons, 319.2 feet length between perpendiculars. Single-screw, triple expansion reciprocating steam engine by the builders. Speed 11½ knots. Withdrawn 1954, broken up 1955.

Zillah Shipping

Founded in 1895 by William Savage of Warrington, the Zillah Shipping & Carrying Co Ltd started with the wooden steamer *Zillah*, both the ship and the company being named after his wife Priscilla. The Savage family had been sailing flat owners but steam meant expansion. In 1906 the company moved to Liverpool and with eight steel coasters, including the *Mayflower* (illustrated), became established in the coal trade to Ireland and the shipment of quarried stone from North Wales to the Mersey.

From 1914 to 1948 Zillah went to the Lytham Shipbuilding & Engineering Co Ltd for new tonnage, the last ship built for them there being the *Hazelfield* (illustrated) in 1948, the year the company was acquired by Coast Lines. Under them Zillah was given a new houseflag (2) but kept the funnel and 'field' names. Motor coasters like the *Fallowfield* (illustrated) replaced the steamers but with the decreasing profitability of coastal tramping Zillah was phased out and ceased to exist by the end of 1967.

1

Many thanks to Roy Fenton and to John Ritchie for furnishing the details for this set.

2

The *Mayflower* was built by Ailsa of Troon in 1905, 370 gross tons, 143.5 feet length between perpendiculars.

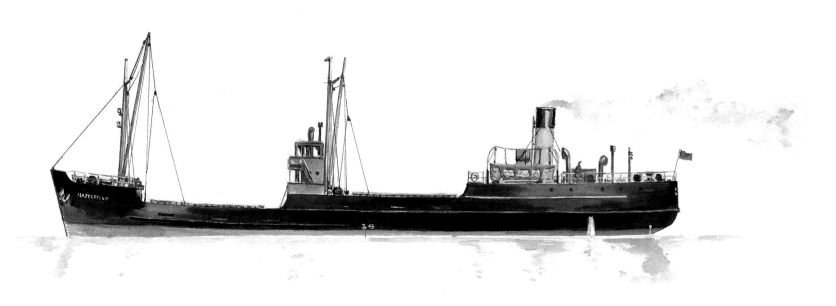

The *Hazelfield* was built by Lytham Shipbuilding & Engineering in 1948, 692 gross tons, 178.4 feet length between perpendiculars.

The *Fallowfield* was built as the *Medusa* by Gebr van Diepen, Waterhuizen, Holland in 1953 and acquired by Zillah the following year, 566 gross tons, 198 feet length overall.

Published by
Landmark Publishing Ltd
Ashbourne Hall, Cokayne Ave, Ashbourne, Derbyshire DE6 1EJ England
Tel: (01335) 347349 Fax: (01335) 347303
e-mail: landmark@clara.net
website: www.landmarkpublishing.co.uk

ISBN 1 84306 185 6

British Library Cataloguing in Publication Data: a catalogue
record for this book is available from the British Library.

Print: Gutenburg Press Ltd, Malta

Design: Mark Titterton

Cover: James Allsopp